ESSENTIAL ELEMENTS

GUITAR ENSEMBLES

EARLY INTERMEDIATE

DISNEY SONGS

D0613495

CONTENTS

Disney characters and artwork © Disney Enterprises, Inc.

Arrangements by Chip Henderson

ISBN 978-1-4584-0087-1

Walt Disney Music Company
Wonderland Music Company, Inc.

DISTRIBUTED BY

HAL•LEONARD®

CORPORATION

7777 W. BLUEMOUND RD. P.O. BOX 13819 MILWAUKEE, WI 53213

In Australia Contact:
Hal Leonard Australia Pty. Ltd.
4 Lentara Court
Cheltenham, Victoria, 3192 Australia
Email: ausadmin@halleonard.com.au

Visit Hal Leonard Online at
www.halleonard.com

THE BARE NECESSITIES

from Walt Disney's THE JUNGLE BOOK

Words and Music by Terry Gilkyson

Verse

Moderately fast

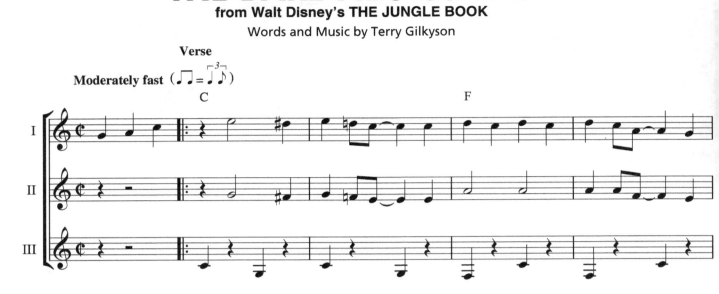

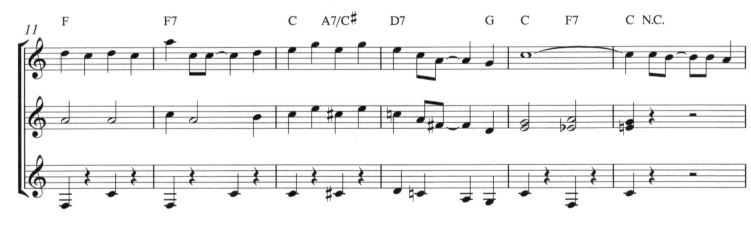

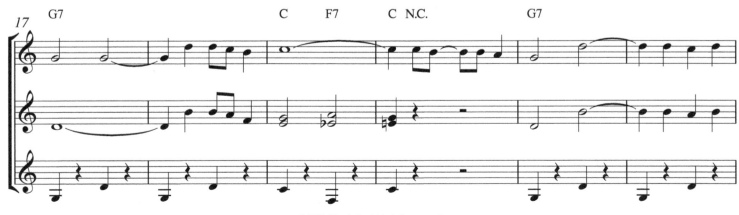

BEAUTY AND THE BEAST

from Walt Disney's BEAUTY AND THE BEAST

Lyrics by Howard Ashman
Music by Alan Menken

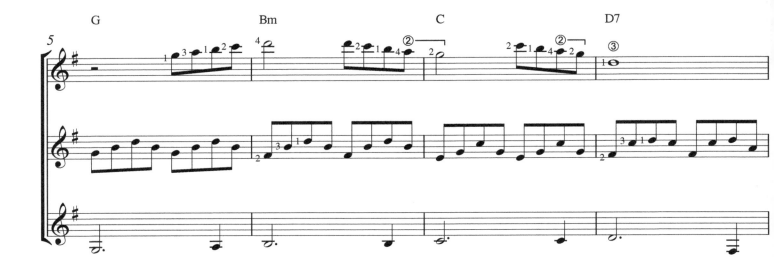

BIBBIDI-BOBBIDI-BOO
(The Magic Song)
from Walt Disney's CINDERELLA

Words by Jerry Livingston
Music by Mack David and Al Hoffman

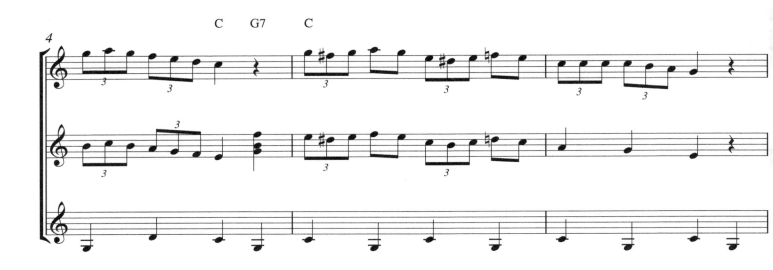

Verse

CAN YOU FEEL THE LOVE TONIGHT

from Walt Disney Pictures' THE LION KING

Music by Elton John
Lyrics by Tim Rice

CHIM CHIM CHER-EE

from Walt Disney's MARY POPPINS

Words and Music by Richard M. Sherman and Robert B. Sherman

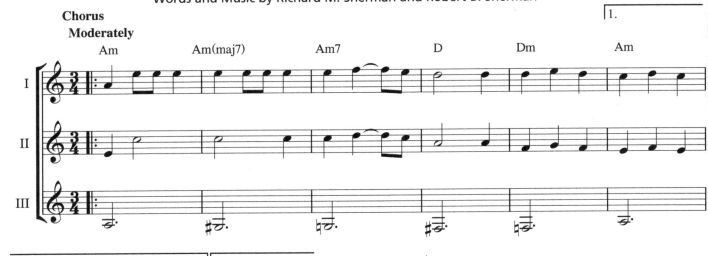

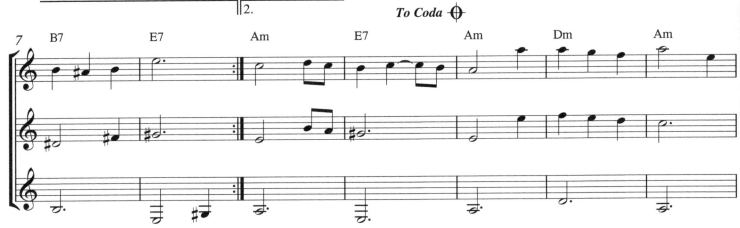

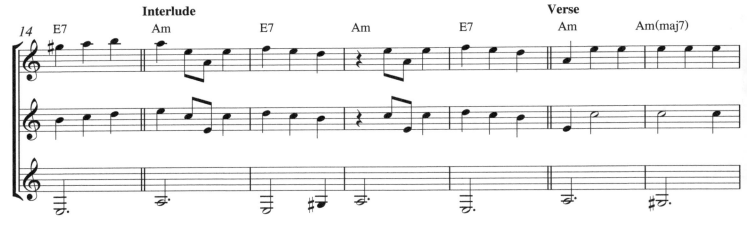

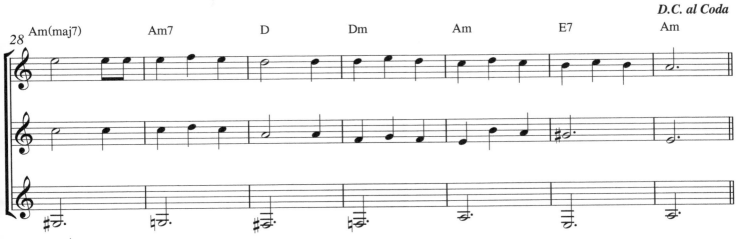

 Coda

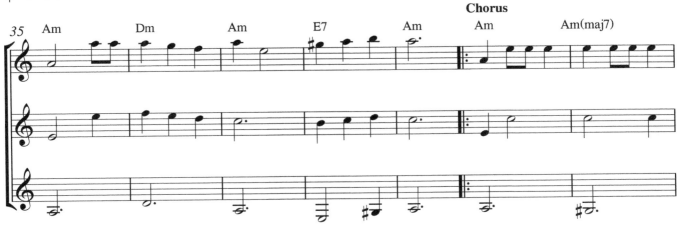

COLORS OF THE WIND

from Walt Disney's POCAHONTAS

Music by Alan Menken
Lyrics by Stephen Schwartz

13

⊕ **Coda**

Chorus

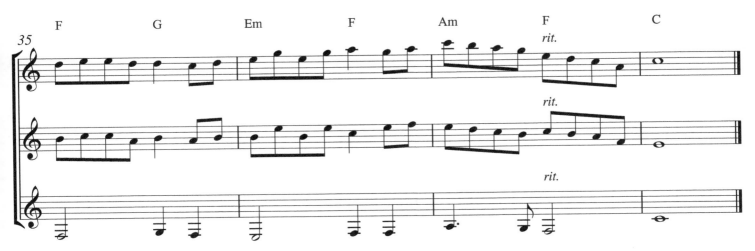

A DREAM IS A WISH YOUR HEART MAKES

from Walt Disney's CINDERELLA

Words and Music by Mack David, Al Hoffman and Jerry Livingston

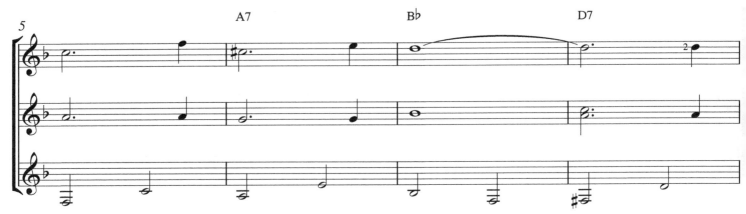

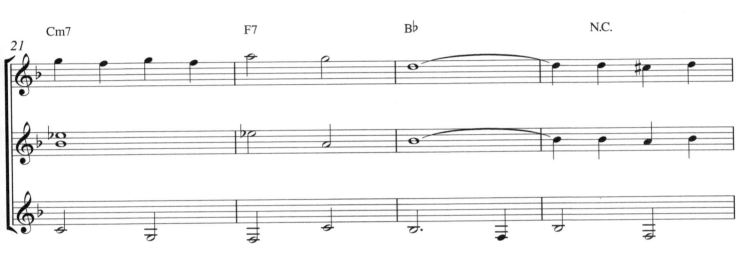

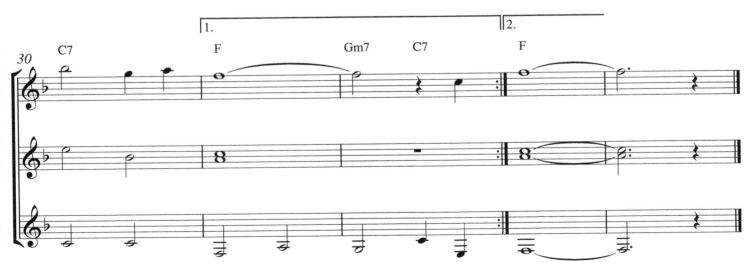

IT'S A SMALL WORLD

from Disneyland Resort® and Magic Kingdom® Park

Words and Music by Richard M. Sherman and Robert B. Sherman

Verse

Moderately fast

Chorus

MICKEY MOUSE MARCH
from Walt Disney's THE MICKEY MOUSE CLUB
Words and Music by Jimmie Dodd

Intro
Moderately, in 2

Verse

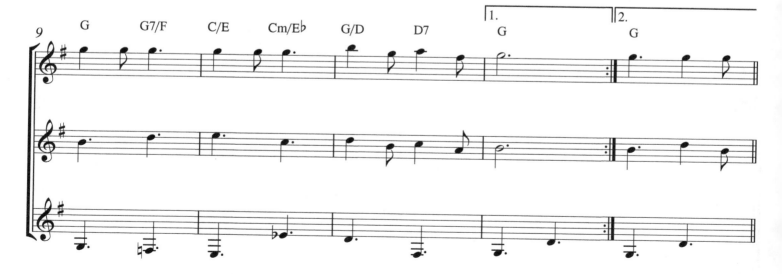

Bridge

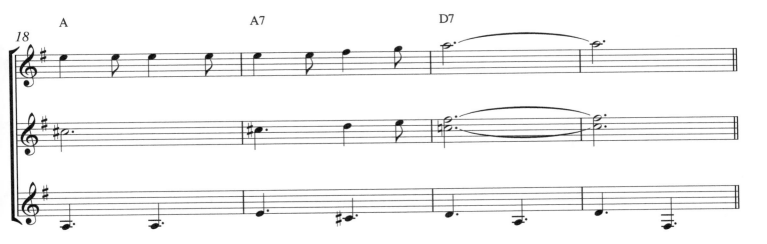

Verse

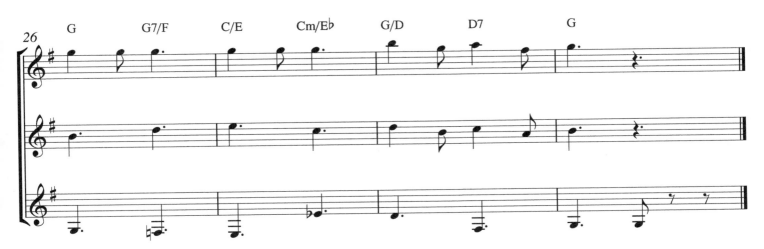

SUPERCALIFRAGILISTICEXPIALIDOCIOUS

from Walt Disney's MARY POPPINS

Words and Music by Richard M. Sherman and Robert B. Sherman

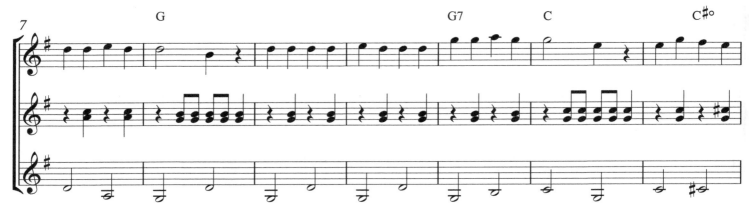

Chorus

YOU'LL BE IN MY HEART
(Pop Version)
from Walt Disney Pictures' TARZAN™

Words and Music by Phil Collins

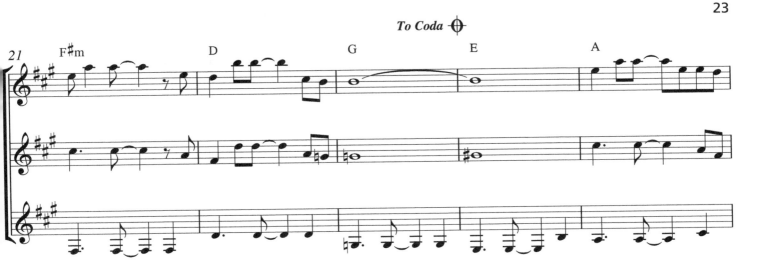

ZIP-A-DEE-DOO-DAH

from Walt Disney's SONG OF THE SOUTH
from Disneyland and Walt Disney World's SPLASH MOUNTAIN

Words by Ray Gilbert
Music by Allie Wrubel

Verse
Moderately

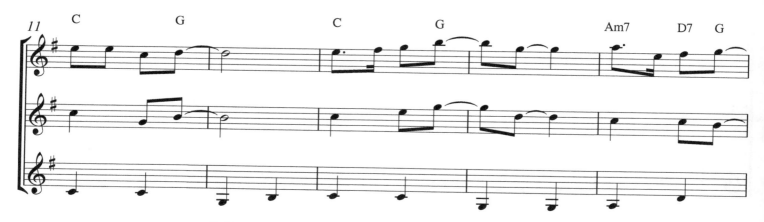

Bridge

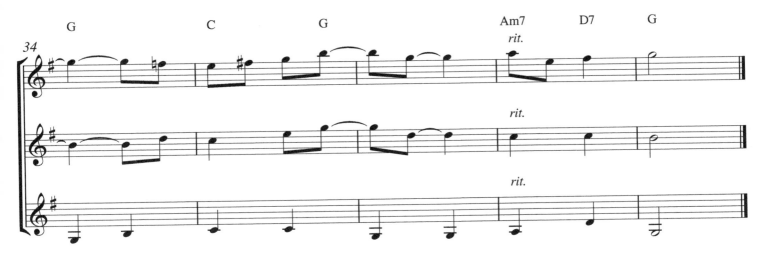

CIRCLE OF LIFE
from Walt Disney Pictures' THE LION KING

Music by Elton John
Lyrics by Tim Rice

Chorus 𝄋

To Coda ⊕

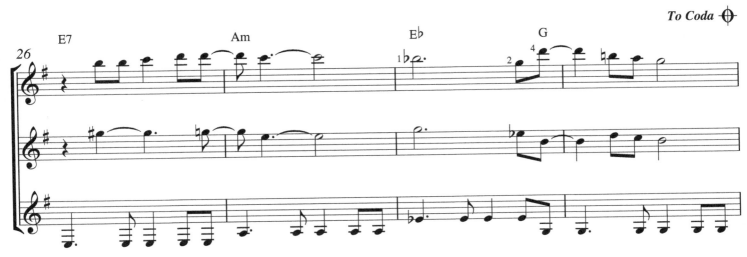

28

D.S. al Coda

Coda

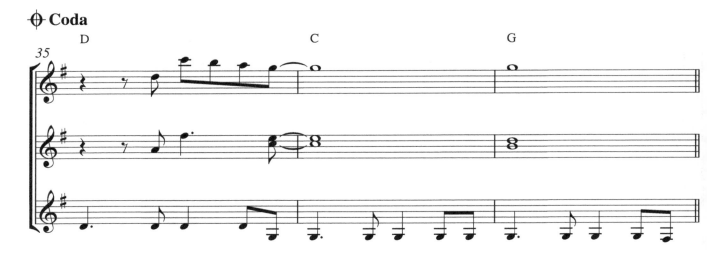

Outro-Chorus

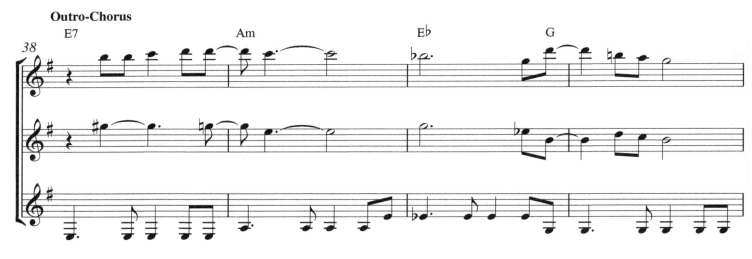

UNDER THE SEA
from Walt Disney's THE LITTLE MERMAID

Music by Alan Menken
Lyrics by Howard Ashman

Intro
Moderately fast

Verse

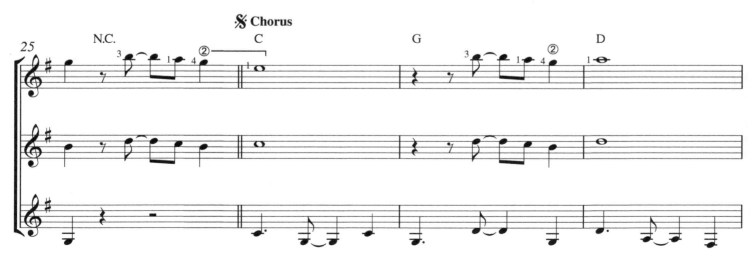

ESSENTIAL ELEMENTS FOR GUITAR

Essential Elements Comprehensive Guitar Method

Take your guitar teaching to a new level! With popular songs in a variety of styles, and quality demonstration and backing tracks on the accompanying online audio, *Essential Elements for Guitar* is a staple of guitar teachers' instruction – and helps beginning guitar students off to a great start. This method was design to meet the National Standards for Music Education, with features such as cross-curricular activities, quizzes, multicultural songs, basic improvisation and more.

BOOK 1   INCLUDES TAB

by Will Schmid and Bob Morris

Concepts covered in Book 1 include: getting started; basic music theory; guitar chords; notes on each string; music history; ensemble playing; performance spotlights; and much more! Songs include: Dust in the Wind • Eleanor Rigby • Every Breath You Take • Hey Jude • Hound Dog • Let It Be • Ode to Joy • Rock Around the Clock • Stand by Me • • Sweet Home Chicago • This Land Is Your Land • You Really Got Me • more!

00862639 Book/Online Audio $19.99
00001173 Book Only $14.99

BOOK 2

by Bob Morris

Concepts taught in Book 2 include: playing melodically in positions up the neck; movable chord shapes up the neck; scales and extended chords in different keys; fingerpicking and pick style; improvisati in positions up the neck; and more! Song include: Auld Lang Syne • Crazy Train • Folsom Prison Blues • La Bamba • Land slide • Nutcracker Suite • Sweet Home Alabama • Your Song • and more.

00865010 Book/Online Audio $22
00120873 Book Only $14

Essential Elements Guitar Ensembles

The songs in the Essential Elements Guitar Ensemble series are playable by three or more guitars. Each arrangement features the melody, a harmony part, and bass line in standard notation along with chord symbols. For groups with more than three or four guitars, the parts can be doubled. This series is perfect for classroom guitar ensembles or other group guitar settings.

Mid-Beginner Level
EASY POP SONGS
00865011/$10.99

CHRISTMAS CLASSICS
00865015/$9.99

CHRISTMAS SONGS
00001136/$10.99

Late Beginner Level
CLASSICAL THEMES
00865005/$10.99

POP HITS
00001128/$12.99

ROCK CLASSICS
00865001/$10.99

Early Intermediate Level
J.S. BACH
00123103/$9.99

THE BEATLES
00172237/$12.99

CHRISTMAS FAVORITES
00128600/$12.99

DISNEY SONGS
00865014/$14.99

IRISH JIGS & REELS
00131525/$9.99

JAZZ BALLADS
00865002/$14.99

MULTICULTURAL SONGS
00160142/$9.99

POPULAR SONGS
00241053/$12.99

TOP SONGS 2010-2019
00295218/$9.99

Mid-Intermediate Level
THE BEATLES
00865008/$14.99

BOSSA NOVA
00865006/$12.99

CHRISTMAS CLASSICS
00865015/$9.99

DUKE ELLINGTON
00865009/$9.99

GREAT THEMES
00865012/$10.99

JIMI HENDRIX
00865013/$9.99

JAZZ STANDARDS
00865007/$14.99

ROCK HITS
00865017/$12.99

ROCK INSTRUMENTALS
00123102/$9.99

TOP HITS
00130606/$9.99

Late Intermediate to Advanced Level
JAZZ CLASSICS
00865016/$9.99

Essential Elements Guitar Songs   INCLUDE TA

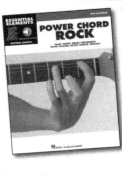

The books in the Essenti Elements Guitar Songs s ries feature popular song selected for the practice of specific guitar chord types. Each book includ eight songs and a CD with fantastic sounding play-along tracks. Prac tice at any tempo with the included Amazing Slow Downer software

BARRE CHORD ROCK
00001137 Late-Beginner Level $12.9

POWER CHORD ROCK
00001139 Mid-Beginner Level $16.9

More Resources

DAILY GUITAR WARM-UPS
by Tom Kolb
Mid-Beginner to Late Intermediate
00865004 Book/Online Audio $14.99

GUITAR FLASH CARDS
96 Cards for Beginning Guitar
00865000...$12.99

HAL•LEONARD®
www.halleonard.com